Life as a
Sunflower

Vic Parker

www.heinemann.co.uk/library
Visit our website to find out more information about Heinemann

To order:
☎ Phone 44 (0) 1865 888066
▤ Send a fax to 44 (0) 1865 314091
▢ Visit the Heinemann Bookshop at www.heinemann.co.uk/library
   catalogue and order online.

First published in Great Britain by Heinemann
Library, Halley Court, Jordan Hill, Oxford
OX2 8EJ, part of Harcourt Education.
Heinemann is a registered trademark of Harcourt
Education Ltd.

Editorial: Jilly Attwood and Claire Throp
Design: Jo Hinton-Malivoire and bigtop,
Bicester, UK
Models made by: Jo Brooker
Picture Research: Catherine Bevan
Production: Séverine Ribierre

Originated by Dot Gradations
Printed and bound in China by South China
Printing Company

ISBN 0 431 17102 5 (hardback)
07 06 05 04 03
10 9 8 7 6 5 4 3 2 1

ISBN 0431 17107 6 (paperback)
07 06 05 04 03
10 9 8 7 6 5 4 3 2 1

British Library Cataloguing in Publication Data
Parker, Vic
Life as a sunflower
583.9'9
A full catalogue record for this book is available
from the British Library.

Acknowledgements
The publishers would like to thank the following
for permission to reproduce photographs:
Andy Purcell pp. **10**, **20**; Bruce Coleman p. **12-13**
(Hans Reinhard); Corbis p. **15** (Renee Lynn); FLPA
pp. **14** (B Borrell), **21** (Albert Visage); Holt Studios
p. **8b** (Nigel Cattlin); Mark N Boulton pp. **4**, **6**, **7**,
8, **9**; NHPA p. **22-23** (Dave Watts); Oxford
Scientific Films p. **18**; OSF p. **19** (Eyal Bartov);
The Garden Picture Library pp. **5** (Juliette Wade),
11 (Chris Burrows), **16**, **17** (Suzie Gibbon).

Cover photograph reproduced with permission of
Photodisc

The publishers would like to thank Annie Davy
for her assistance in the preparation of this book.

Every effort has been made to contact copyright
holders of any material reproduced in this book.
Any omissions will be rectified in subsequent
printings if notice is given to the publishers.

Contents

Seed surprise

Here are some small stripy seeds.

4

Can you guess what they will grow into?

Into the earth

Plant the seeds to see what will happen.

Don't forget to give them plenty of water.

Root and shoot

Long roots start growing under the ground.

One day, a spiky green shoot appears.

Soon, leaves begin to sprout.

Into bud

The weather becomes warmer.

A bud bulges at the top
of the shoot.

bud

Can you guess what will happen?

Bloom time

One day it suddenly opens into a **big**, beautiful sunflower!

Visitors arrive

Busy bumble bees **bu**zz around the sunflower.

Buzz! Buzz!

Butterflies flutter by too.

15

Sunflower power

The sunflower rises **higher** and **higher**.

When the weather turns colder, the sunflower head nods and droops.

The wind shakes the sunflower and its seeds fall to the ground.

Near and far

Some seeds lie where they are.

Birds fly off with other seeds.

Next year
the seeds will
grow into ...

21

Lots of new sunflowers!

Index

The end

Notes for adults

The **Life as a** . . . series looks at the life cycles of familiar animals and plants, introducing the young child to the concept of change over time. There are four titles in the series and when used together, they will enable comparison of similarities and differences between life cycles. The key curriculum early learning goals relevant to this series are:

Knowledge and understanding of the world
- find out about, and identify, some features of living things that the young child observes
- ask questions about why things happen
- differentiate between past and present.

This book takes the reader on a circular journey from the beginning of a sunflower's life as a seed, through its developmental stages (including where and what it needs to grow), to maturity and reproduction. The book will help children extend their vocabulary, as they will hear new words such as *root*, *shoot* and *bud*. You might like to introduce the word *petal*, or the word *wilt* (when reading to children that the sunflower starts to droop when the weather turns colder).

Additional information about sunflowers

Plants differ from animals in that they make their own food. Each sunflower seed contains a young plant in embryo form and a store of food for the embryo's growth. Roots then anchor the plant in the ground and draw up water and minerals. A green substance in the leaves (called chlorophyll) combines energy from sunlight with carbon dioxide (from the air) and water to make food (and surplus oxygen). The flower is where the reproductive parts of the plant are found. The stems of sunflowers turn so the flowers can always face the Sun. As well as being grown for their beauty, sunflowers are farmed for food. Sunflower seeds contain large amounts of vitamins. They can be eaten as a snack, or used to produce oil for cooking and making into margarine.

Follow-up activities

- Plant some sunflower seeds in spring. Watch them grow, measuring their height week by week.
- Use some sunflower seeds and glue, with crayons or paints, to make a picture of a sunflower.
- Make a height chart of a fully-grown sunflower (about 2.5m high). Mark the readers' heights against it.